MR. DREAM CLEAN

Rodney McGilvery
Mr. Dream Clean

All rights reserved
Copyright © 2024 by Rodney McGilvery

No part of this publication may be reproduced, distributed, or transmitted in
any form or by any means, including photocopying, recording, or other
electronic or mechanical methods, without the prior written permission of the
publisher, except in the case of brief quotations embodied in critical reviews
and certain other noncommercial uses permitted by copyright law.

—

Published by - Spines
ISBN: 979-8-89383-158-0

MR. DREAM CLEAN

RODNEY McGILVERY

CONTENTS

Introduction   7

 1. Who in your business is important?   11
 2. What type of customer is out there?   14
 3. My Cleaning Supplies Approach   16
 4. Residential vs Commercial Business   20
 5. Networking   24
 6. How to develop Referral Partners   29
 7. Purchase vs Lease for a Company Vehicle   33
 8. Corporate Social Responsibility (CSR)   36
 9. The Importance of Being Unavailable   41
10. Work-Life Balance   45
11. Is your Business Sellable?   49
    Understanding Your Business   53
12. What is HR?   54
13. Employee vs Independent Contractor (W2 vs
    1099)   64
14. Business Structure   67
15. Beneficial Ownership Information (BOI)   77
16. Insurance & Bonds   81
17. Licenses and Registrations   85
18. Certifications   90

Conclusion   95

Introduction

When I meet people, I have not seen in a while, they always ask me, "Do you still have that cleaning business?" The one I started back in 1999, people and friends thought I was crazy. Here I sit and think, was it that crazy of an idea?

I was born in rural Mississippi to my mother, a schoolteacher, and my father, a police officer. All of my grandparents were farmers and hunters to help support the family. My parents helped me with the first newspaper route in our neighborhood at age 10. I also had a bicycle repair shop for kids' bicycles and sold juice cups in front of our house. Coming from a religious background, I was also taught that if there was anything you wanted, you had to work hard to get it. The entrepreneurial spirit has always been a part of my life, and as a kid, my parents taught us that hard work produces results. As a family member said many times before, "We don't have a lot of money, but there is nothing that we can't get."

After graduating high school, I attended college at the University of Southern Mississippi in my hometown. Upon graduating from college, I moved to Louisiana to become a manager at a grocery store I had worked at since I was a kid. My mom and dad stayed in our hometown; they traveled but never moved anywhere else. They encouraged me to get out there and see the world. With every job I ever had, I exceeded all expectations. After joining the military, I continued to excel by graduating from the top of my class in every military course I attended. After leaving the Army, I moved to Miami. I continued working as a computer specialist, which I had dreamed of. Later, I managed a health club and worked at several clubs in Miami Beach.

The entrepreneurial spirit led me to start a business that I had a passion for - Cleaning and Organizing - which was instilled in me my entire life. Every family member was not surprised that I started a cleaning business and have been continuing it for the past 24 years. Here we are today!

And YES, I still have that Cleaning Business!

I want to share the details of how I started, maintained, grew, and profited from having a cleaning business. Certain levels of education can and may help develop a business, but it does not prevent someone without formal education from being able to start and run a successful business. Every business is a process. The process is a day-by-day education to move from one level to the next level of business. I will give you a guide, that has benefited Dream Clean and catapulted us from one level to the next, which continues today.

It's essential to have a plan, whether it is a one-year or a twenty-year plan. It's critical to have a vision for your business's future. Dream Clean has been in business for 24 years now, and we always have a plan for what to do as a business. As a small business, it can be challenging to navigate dealing with the government and becoming certified as an SBE and DBE. However, your county makes it easy by doing workshops so you all can learn and use this information.

Qualifications like SBE and DBE can help you stand out and grow your business. When it comes to effectively managing a business, a number of tasks are crucial for success. One such task is staying up-to-date on the latest software solutions that can help streamline operations and improve productivity. Attending industry conferences and networking events is essential for staying current with industry trends and expanding professional networks. It also allows you to gain new perspectives, learn from others, and potentially form valuable relationships. By working with other companies, you can tap into their expertise and resources, which can help you grow and expand your business. Attending networking events can help you connect with like-minded individuals who can offer support and advice. We do a lot of collaboration and networking with other companies. We give them direction and learn new ideas from them.

Additionally, maintaining detailed records and being diligent with bookkeeping can help ensure that finances are managed effectively and accurately. These tasks require particular focus and dedication, but the payoff can be significant regarding overall business success. We can ensure that Dream Clean is always on top of our finances and making wise decisions for the future. All these free business development resources are available throughout your city, including help with certifications, networking opportunities, bonding, loan needs, and information about jobs in your trade.

The upcoming chapters will list essential items and provide a reference list of what is necessary to start a business.

This book is a reference and guide to starting, growing, and expanding your business. Enjoy!

WHO IN YOUR BUSINESS IS IMPORTANT?

Employees are the most important aspect of the company. Onboarding employees and discovering what is important to each individual is the catalyst in having a successful relationship. When you communicate in the very beginning to your employee what's important to the company then you can also solicit the employee to share this idea.

Cross-training employees is also a very important part. Your staff are not machines and they do have private emergencies or get sick. Who is to do their job? That is when cross training comes in. The staff needs to know what other team members are doing and can jump in to do someone else's job. You might be surprised. You might just have found a new supervisor! In today's world, most things are very technology driven and most people know about computers and different software. Expand your employee's work tasks by adding clerical work, e.g. supply inventory, writing the schedule, show them how to create the estimates. As we reach out to sell our business to customers and widen their view on what our capabilities are. Employees have aspirations of doing more in the future.

Regular training should cover a range of essential aspects, such as:
- Effective customer communication
- Proper on-site procedures
- Correct handling of cleaning solutions
- Efficient cleaning techniques
- Operation of various machines and more.

Teaching and educating your employees never ends. The job environment keeps changing and we need to adapt to it.

Don't just say something important ONCE. Research has shown that you need to reiterate tasks about 7 times until the message sinks in.

Teaching and continually asking questions about family, the future, and vacations. You will start to develop an idea and it's important that the business know, what is also important to them.

The future and health are very important aspects. We have a vision for the business and we need to create a vision for the employees to create and understand the vision. If the staff can see a great future they are excited because it's their future too. To inspire and create change takes the business to the next level. Teaching an employee more about the business is a catalyst for you as a business owner to move from working in your business to move to work on your business instead. When an employee has gone through all the aspects of your business and their job performance is great, it can be beneficial for you to help that employee create their own business. You are not just creating a bigger and better life for your employee but you're also creating an ally or a Referral Partner.

Creating a Referral Partner from a former employee has taken us to a level. I never could imagine. A relationship with past employees is always beneficial to have because they say something good about your company. It never dawned on me the impact that this may have until I started hearing from a potential new customer that they were referred to us by a former employee. Receiving a new applicant in the office, who was referred by a former employee. Having a past employee come to the office for a coffee, tea, or get-together as a business owner. This lets me know that I'm doing the right thing.

Communication is the key to many aspects of life as well as in business. Always keep your communication open with your employees and customers. Great communication and great listening will let you know what works, what doesn't work, and what we need to work on. Always keep your employees as the most important aspect of your company!

What Type of Customer Is Out There?

Remember- not all size fits all. It's important to remember that not all solutions work for everyone. While you may have various services available, it's crucial to customize them to meet each client's needs. Feel free to make adjustments or modifications, as this will ensure that your services fit your clients perfectly.

Listening is important when it comes to serving your clients. Allow them to express themselves fully. Even if the issue seems familiar, it is essential to let the customer articulate their needs and concerns. It's crucial to acknowledge and comprehend their needs. Inquire further to gain a complete understanding of their objectives.

Regarding customer service, nonverbal communication is just as important as verbal communication. Some clients may have a wish list but need more financial resources. In such cases, how do you proceed? We recommend asking the client about their budget. Inform them that a written estimate will be sent and detail precisely what can be accomplished within their budget. Offer options for additional services from the list and establish the cost for future service visits to achieve their desired end goal.

The "Serve, Don't Sell" philosophy is crucial here. Your main objective is not to make a sale or persuade the client. Instead, your focus should be to serve them in the best possible way. To determine how you can be of service, you need to establish a relationship of trust. When considering budget constraints, assessing whether a short-term solution or long-term commitment would be more suitable for the individual or organization. While generating revenue is a key objective for any business, offering mutually beneficial pricing is essential. Asking questions can help determine whether the focus is on a temporary arrangement or building a lasting partnership. Investing in a long-term relationship can ultimately lead to more significant financial gain.

It is important to be cautious about your business deals and agreements. You should know your capabilities and only agree to sell something you can confidently deliver.

Know who YOU are - not all money is good money.

My Cleaning Supplies Approach

The janitor's closet offers many cleaning supplies, and with so many options, it's easy for your cleaning staff to get confused. With a different solution for every cleaning task, they're left with a dilemma. What's the best product for cleaning floors? Can solutions meant for restrooms also be used in the kitchen?

When it comes to cleaning, you don't need many different products. Just stick to the basics: glass cleaner, degreaser, disinfectant, and floor cleaner. Before using any product, know what it can and cannot do. Never mix cleaning products, as this can be dangerous. If a product is too strong, you can always dilute it. Lastly, always research before using any chemicals, as they can be hazardous depending on their function.

According to OSHA (Occupational Safety and Health Administration) and the EPA (Environmental Protection Agency), there are three distinct types of cleaning products: cleaners, sanitizers, and disinfectants.

- **Cleaners** – Help remove dirt by scrubbing/wiping
- **Sanitizers** – Use chemicals to reduce viruses and bacteria on the surface of items
- **Disinfectants** – Use chemicals to destroy microorganisms that cause infection

By categorizing cleaning products, you can quickly identify hazardous chemicals and determine which chemicals are present in specific products. Knowing the substances in each product helps you use them safely and effectively and clean more efficiently with the right cleaning solution for each job. Mixing cleaning chemicals is a big no-no. It's not only dangerous to combine them, but keeping them separate reduces the risk of making a mistake. It's important to avoid accidentally grabbing laundry detergent when you're looking for a heavy-duty, all-purpose cleaner.

It's crucial to choose the right cleaning chemical for the job. Selecting the wrong one could cause costly damage to surfaces and finishes or produce unsatisfactory results. Picking the correct cleaning agent can seem daunting, especially if you need clarification on how much to use or which one is best suited for the job. However, with this guide to cleaning chemicals, you can break down the chemistry behind cleaning and discover the best practices for various products and applications.

Cleaning solutions contain a variety of different ingredients to break down, capture, and remove soils. The most common are called surface active agents, also known as surfactants. These ingredients change the surface tension of water, increasing its spreading and wetting properties. Cleaning products include many other chemicals, including sequestering agents, builders, solvents, fragrances, preservatives, and dyes. Most importantly, they also include pH adjusters. These additives tune the product's pH, allowing it to capture better and remove specific kinds of soils.

Maintaining a clean and healthy environment requires distinct cleaning, sanitizing, and disinfecting methods. Cleaning involves removing dirt and germs from surfaces and objects. Sanitizing requires using specialized products that destroy almost all bacteria on a surface within 30 seconds. Disinfecting consists of using a disinfectant to eliminate all living organisms. Antimicrobial pesticides, such as sanitizers and disinfectants, are under the scrutiny of EPA regulations. Both require a thorough cleaning of surfaces before application, as germs can hide under dirt, reducing their germ-killing effectiveness. Sanitizers are particularly useful for surfaces that get in contact with food. Disinfectants are most effective on non-porous surfaces such as restroom fixtures, porcelain tile, and food preparation and storage areas. However, it's important to note that some disinfectants, including bleach, can be harsh on the skin and eyes and cause irritation. Cleaning chemicals are necessary to keep interiors clean and hygienic, but they can also pose health and environmental risks. The Environmental Protection Agency (EPA) cautions that these products may contain irritants that can harm the skin, eyes, or respiratory system. Additionally, the concentrated forms of these chemicals may be classified as hazardous, which can create potential issues with handling, storage, and disposal. Fortunately, the EPA suggests using green cleaning products can help reduce human health and environmental concerns. To make it easier for consumers to choose safer and more sustainable cleaning options, the nonprofit organization Green Seal has established strict standards for product performance, sustainability, and health. Selecting products that meet these standards lets you clean your home or office confidently and safely.

When it comes to chemical safety, there are some fundamental principles that you should keep in mind. These include using common sense, exercising patience, acquiring knowledge, and taking responsibility. Even if you don't work with cleaning chemicals, having a solid grasp of these basic principles can go a long way in preventing accidents and avoiding mistakes. So, it's always a good idea to educate yourself about the safe handling of chemicals and be mindful of the potential risks.

Residential vs Commercial Business

To make a well-informed decision about hiring a cleaning service, it's necessary to understand the differences between residential and commercial cleaning. The technology, techniques, and methods used for cleaning are distinct and unique, which is why it's important to know what sets them apart. Maintaining a clean and sanitized environment is crucial for both residential and commercial areas, as it promotes well-being and encourages people to maintain cleanliness in their surroundings. While both cleaning services share the same goal of ensuring a clean and healthy environment, there are key differences and duties between them that we will outline for you. By understanding these distinctions, you can make an informed decision about which cleaning service will best suit your needs.

What is Commercial Cleaning?

Commercial cleaners hired by business owners, organizations, or companies perform commercial cleaning services. Commercial cleaning companies are contracted for cleaning tasks on various premises, including schools, offices, commercial kitchens, industrial, medical, healthcare facilities, hotels, restaurants, warehouses, movie theaters, malls, and entertainment centers.

The scope of work and duties of a commercial cleaning company typically involves general cleaning and routines. Commercial cleaning services are dedicated to cleaning tiles, furniture, windows, washing facilities, and ceilings. A commercial cleaner ensures that all offices in a building, an entire warehouse, and all rooms in a school are cleaned thoroughly.

What is Residential Cleaning?

Residential cleaning is a specialized service that tidies homes and other living spaces. However, the quality of the technology, processes, and training residential cleaners use can vary depending on the provider. A residential cleaner can work for a cleaning company or be self-employed.

When you hire a professional residential cleaning company, you can expect a top-notch customer experience and quality service. Residential cleaners are experts at putting everything in its place to make your home look fantastic, leaving your visitors feeling impressed.

The Difference between Commercial and Residential Cleaning

Effective cleaning services are crucial for maintaining a clean and hygienic environment in settings such as businesses, offices, homes, schools, and medical centers. These services can generally be classified into two main categories: commercial and residential cleaning. You can either undertake the cleaning tasks yourself or seek the assistance of a professional.

Are you curious about the distinctions between commercial and residential cleaning services? Here are some explanations of how these two types differ.

Area of Coverage

Commercial and residential cleaning services have a distinct point of difference: the area and space they cover. Commercial cleaning services require more because they cover larger areas, while residential cleaning services are relatively more accessible due to the smaller areas they cover.

The Process of Cleaning

The cleaning process for commercial and residential properties varies significantly. Residential cleaning is generally straightforward, while commercial cleaning involves more complex tasks that are often split up. Companies and businesses have established their cleaning guidelines and procedures, because cleaning in a hotel is different from cleaning in a school, and cleaning in a home is different from cleaning in an office.

Cleaning Standards

The safety and health standards for every company and business vary by state and municipality. As a result, commercial cleaning services and companies must comply with the regulations of their respective state. On the other hand, residential cleaning services are set by homeowners, who may not be aware of the standards that your business must adhere to.

Cleaning Supplies and Equipment

One key distinction between commercial and residential cleaning lies in their respective scale. Commercial cleaning, in particular, involves larger areas requiring more cleaning tools, devices, and equipment than the typical residential cleaners. As such, commercial cleaners often rely on industrial-grade vacuum cleaners, floor polishers, and other powerful machinery that can effectively tackle cleaning tasks in hotels, offices, medical centers, and hospitals, resulting in superior outcomes.

Networking

Using your personal and business connections to get advice for your business or attract new customers and vendors is known as business networking. Numerous well-known business networking organizations have developed networking event models. Business networking promotes a mutually beneficial relationship between business people and potential clients or customers. The benefits of business networking are intangible and include communication with other professionals and industry-related interactions.

In small businesses, a business owner's networking efforts often yield the most significant results. Sharing knowledge is the most advantageous of the many potential gains to be made from networking. To enjoy the benefits of a network, it is crucial to understand the advantages of business networking, and how it can help increase sales, improve efficiency, and morale, and build brand awareness for your business.

What Is Business Networking?

Business networking involves interacting with other business owners, potential suppliers, or professionals with business expertise to expand your business. You gain access to diverse individuals through networking, including competitors and clients. You can offer them something of value, such as advice, knowledge, services, or contacts, in exchange for their expertise.

As a business owner, fostering relationships and assisting others offers more than the possibility of gaining clients or generating referrals. Networking provides a means of discovering prospects for partnerships, joint ventures, or new avenues for your enterprise to expand. The wisdom gathered from these experiences of others can prove to be an invaluable asset before committing your time and resources to a particular venture.

How Does Business Networking Work?

Attending networking events or local business luncheons provides an opportunity to connect with individuals in similar situations who are also working to grow their businesses. These events aim to introduce new concepts and techniques while serving as a platform for local business people to meet and exchange ideas. When meeting someone, exchanging business cards and following up later to discuss any points or topics in your conversation is essential. If the other party initiates the discussion, you can share information, seek knowledge, or exchange business contacts.

Most business people are optimistic, and frequent interaction with such people can be a great morale boost, particularly during the challenging early stages of a new business. You'll discover that many, if not all, business owners have experienced similar ownership challenges. A large portion of local business is still conducted on a handshake basis, and the most effective way to network with other local business owners and entrepreneurs is by attending face-to-face meetings and local business groups. Attend your networking group's meetings regularly and be ready to contribute something valuable to the group. Pick the networking medium that suits you best.

What Are the Benefits of Business Networking?

By engaging in business networking, you may raise awareness of or stay current with your industry's latest trends or technology. Your network can also provide professional mentors or contacts to assist you with any challenges. For instance, if you need a bookkeeper, accountant, or lawyer for your business, you can find the perfect candidate through your network. Similarly, you can use networking channels to locate an angel investor or venture capitalist if you require equity financing.

Networking is an excellent way to broaden your knowledge by benefiting from the perspectives and previous experiences of others. For example, if you are considering exporting your products or services, you can obtain valuable advice from someone who has previously conducted comparable international business.

Networking instills confidence in the competitiveness and comparability of your company and the methods you have implemented to manage and operate it compared to similar businesses.

Types of Business Networking

While attending events, keep an eye out for potential business opportunities where you can offer something and benefit in return. This might involve discussing market conditions and industry trends that affect both businesses. By working together, you can develop a better understanding of the market that you both operate in.

Business Seminars

Consider seeking out and participating in business seminars to develop new professional connections. Cultivating these relationships with your peers and associates is crucial, and maintaining regular communication can help ensure you all remain up-to-date. When it comes to effective networking, listening is critical. Prioritizing how you can assist the person you are engaging with, rather than focusing solely on how they can benefit you, is a fundamental aspect of establishing a mutually beneficial relationship.

Networking Groups

Influential business networking groups serve as platforms for exchanging business insights, ideas, and mutual support. Nowadays, a multitude of online groups provide networking services and communities. An excellent example of a large networking group or site is the Chamber of Commerce in your city, which can help bring professionals together

Professional Associations

Groups of individuals with shared interests and professions come together to form organizations. These groups may require membership fees or specific qualifications, but they can be invaluable for entrepreneurs seeking to broaden their connections. Consider beginning your networking journey at the Chamber of Commerce in your locality.

Key Takeaways

Business networking allows business people to collaborate with other experts to help them grow their businesses or improve their professional lives. The benefits of business networking include:

- Opportunities to help other business owners
- Receiving assistance from other owners
- Additional knowledge and perspective
- Communication with like-minded individuals

How to develop Referral Partners

When expanding your business, a referral partner program can be a game-changer. It's no secret that referred customers tend to have higher conversion rates and are more inclined to become long-term customers. But with referral partners, you can take this idea to the next level. Our comprehensive guide will equip you with all the knowledge you need to establish successful referral partnerships and generate leads. By building up your network and taking the time to understand the strengths and interests of those in your circle, you'll naturally create a strong referral partnership network.

What Is a Referral Partner?

An individual or business that recommends your brand, products, or services to their customers is called a referral partner. Over time, this connection can result in mutual referrals that help to increase sales revenue.

Referral partnerships are a great way to expand your reach beyond your typical customer referral program. Let's explore this in detail: referral partners have unique qualities. They already have established relationships with the people they plan to refer. They have the potential to send many referrals to your business. Additionally, they have a direct relationship with you and your brand. They might personally know you, appreciate your product or service, and act as natural ambassadors.

Benefits of a Referral Partner Program

Having one or more referral partnerships can significantly impact the success of your business. There are several reasons for this:

1. Referral partners are made aware only after they successfully close a deal, which means the overall cost of acquiring customers through referrals is lower than other channels.
2. Referral partners search and prospect leads for you, making the sales cycle shorter. When the leads are introduced to your business, they are already familiar with it, allowing you to focus on closing the sale. This also helps build trust and makes it easier to close larger accounts.
3. Referral partnerships provide access to new customers that may have yet to be reachable. Referral partners have an established community and have already earned the trust of these potential customers. As their business grows, your business can also gain access to these potential customers.

4. Referral partnerships can generate numerous leads and conversations, increasing reach and visibility. This approach can work exceptionally well if referral partners are incentivized with a relationship that also works for them.
5. Referral partnerships promote a sense of belonging among customers, leading to improved customer retention. Referred customers are more likely to conduct repeat business and have a higher lifetime value.

We have found that the number one way is to be a part of the Chamber of Commerce in your city. Chambers of Commerce are committed to maintaining a strong presence in your community. The Chamber of Commerce focuses on the involvement of its members, which makes it stronger. Every chamber will have a committee that closely suits something you're good at in your business. A Chamber of Commerce can be a catalyst to answer business questions through technical assistance. They can also help with your marketing, your publications, your communication, and material, and a chamber will have a minority and a small business manager to help you with your business needs or refer you to someone who can. This organization can help connect you with someone else in the chamber that you can possibly do business with you. They can also assist you in knowing what's happening in the community and also keep you informed on grants and loans that you may qualify for, can keep you on track with growth, educate and push your development in your business. Here are some of the committees: construction, education, health, and wellness international trade, marketing public relations, membership, and women's council. The more you put into an organization, the more you will get out of the organization (GEK). As we approach the idea of how to develop Referral Partners, it is an everyday approach to have relationships as your number one priority when it comes to development Referral Partners. Change will be something that's imminent. Change is learning.

When it comes to developing referral partners, building lasting relationships should be your top priority. Keep your referral partners informed of any changes in your business, including new focus areas. Changes are inevitable, and learning from them is essential. By bringing your referral partners along your business journey, you can help create more referral partners. This system will create continuous daily marketing for your business. Referral partners only refer people with whom they have built a personal connection. This pre-existing relationship makes it easier to close sales since people trust the referral source and are more willing to investigate your product or service, ultimately leading to purchases. This results in higher-quality leads and customers likely to stick around for extended periods. As a result, there is a higher customer retention rate and an increased average customer lifetime value even though the lead pool might be smaller since partners only recommend it to people they know; the trust factor and quality more than make up for it.

PURCHASE VS LEASE FOR A COMPANY VEHICLE

When is it better to buy a car?

Purchasing a car instead of leasing it is a financially wise decision. Moreover, it might suit your driving patterns and personal preferences. Let's take a look at some scenarios where buying a car would be a preferable option.

You're focused on long-term value.

Investing in a car means acquiring a depreciating asset. Unless you have the cash, you will need to get a car loan and pay interest, but you will gain full vehicle ownership. You can sell or trade it anytime and clear the remaining loan balance. Moreover, once you pay off the loan, you can keep driving your car without worrying about monthly payments.

Leasing a car can be an excellent way to pay less each month, but it means you won't own the vehicle. However, leasing with an option to buy doesn't necessarily guarantee a good deal. Negotiating with the dealer and auto loan lender to lower the monthly payments when buying can be a good strategy. Saving money is possible by reducing the purchase price and exploring the best interest rates available. For a long-term lease (over 36 months), you may have lower monthly payments than a shorter one. However, the car's value is likely to plummet after this period, meaning you'll be overpaying without the advantage of gaining any ownership.

You have 10% to 20% to put down.

It's generally recommended to have a down payment of at least 20% if you're buying a new car and 10% for a used one. This will help you ensure you'll get a lower interest rate and monthly payments. Plus, you'll be less likely to end up "underwater" on your loan (or owning more than your car is worth). Understandably, coming up with 10% or 20% can be significant. Fortunately, with a car lease, there's no need for a large down payment. Plus, you may not need to put down any money if you have good credit.

You drive a lot.

If you have a long daily commute or drive a lot for any other reason, purchasing a car might be better. Usually, under a leasing contract, you'll have a mileage limit of 10,000 to 15,000 miles per year. If you exceed the limit, you can be charged over 20 cents per each additional mile you put on the car. These charges can add up rather quickly.

You want to customize your car.

It's a priority for some drivers to make their car feel like their own by customizing it. When buying a vehicle, you're free to do with it as you please, from adding a turbocharger to painting your car neon green (a questionable choice — but you have every right). A leased car isn't likely to allow you such freedoms. While your lessor might agree to certain modifications, you'll still need to return the vehicle to its original state before bringing it back at the end of the lease.

When is it better to lease a car?

Leasing a car is similar to having a subscription with an end date. You can use the vehicle for as long as you pay for it. Although not building any equity in the vehicle may be a drawback, a car lease can still be a better option in specific scenarios.

Bottom line

Over the long run, continually leasing is more expensive than buying a car. Plus, purchasing a vehicle allows you to build equity in an asset. At the same time, there are situations where leasing still makes sense — after all, it's usually more accessible on your monthly budget. Review your priorities and do the math to determine what works best for you.

Corporate Social Responsibility (CSR)

What is Corporate Social Responsibility?

Corporate social responsibility (CSR) is a form of self-regulation in business that aims to ensure social accountability and positively impact society. Companies can adopt CSR by prioritizing environmental sustainability and being conscious of their environmental impact, promoting diversity, equality, and inclusion in the workplace, treating their employees with dignity and Respect, giving back to the community, and making ethical business decisions.

At Dream Clean, we have long embraced Social Responsibility as a key value of our organization; it has been a foundational part of our corporate culture for over 24 years to continually weigh the impact of our business on the people in whatever we do.

Social Responsibility is on an equal footing with our values of Integrity – which speaks to the fairness and honesty with which we conduct our business, and the trust granted us by the public – and Respect, which is our concern for the well-being of our employees and our relationships with service partners and suppliers.

We will continue building upon its commitment to be a socially responsible corporation with a long-term objective of incorporating corporate social Responsibility into every touch-point and strive to be a leader in corporate social responsibility through leadership in community outreach and environmental efforts.

As residents of this country, we are also charged with protecting the greatest place on earth, by which we have a vested interest in the sustainability of its economy, environment, and people. Our CSR initiatives focus on three areas: Environmental, Economic, and Social.

Corporate Social Responsibility is the business of every employee. Each individual has an important role in defining CSR through their day-to-day work and inspiring and challenging the organization to do more.

Establishing a culture of accountability and transformation must begin with your organization. To initiate this process, engaging the younger, environmentally mindful workforce in innovative Corporate Social Responsibility projects is beneficial. A dedicated group of employees who bring passion to such initiatives can spark a healthy competitive spirit and opportunities for appreciation.

In today's competitive business environment, employees seek jobs that offer financial security, autonomy, meaning, and opportunities for development and advancement. Employees also want time to pursue personal interests and enjoy time outside of the workplace. Responding to these needs is nothing new, and we are committed to creating a supportive, flexible work environment while providing services that help the employees in their lives outside of work.

Committing to creating a supportive, flexible work environment that gives employees more control over their work is an important means to achieve greater work/life balance and enhanced productivity. Employees have said that balancing their responsibilities for work, family, education, and other commitments is becoming increasingly difficult under traditional work schedules. Their ability to address work and family is critical in their decision to stay.

To address these employee and business needs, we have developed five flexibility principles:

1. **The enterprise doesn't stop:** The enterprise never stops working. Somewhere in the world, your employee(s) are working on solutions for your clients. That does not mean all employees work 24/7 and 365 days a year.
2. **Balancing of needs:** Flexibility encompasses how, where, and when work gets done. Commit to providing your employees the greatest degree of

flexibility while balancing the needs of your clients, our business, our teams, and individual employees.

3. **Trust and personal responsibility:** Consistent with our core value of "trust and personal responsibility in all relationships," We expect managers and employees to make decisions, including those about flexibility options, consistent with this value and to demonstrate personal responsibility to ensure business commitments.

4. **Range of options:** Flexible work options are a vehicle to meet the needs of your clients and can be employee or management-initiated. However, all options must be management approved. Open dialog is important to understand and secure support for the most flexible option, which may include varied work times, part-time, job-share, work from home, etc, depending on the needs of the business division, client, or individual employee.

5. **Understanding differences:** Operating effectively in the "new world of work", and in a globally integrated enterprise, requires sensitivity to a broad range of differences. This requires every employee to exercise care and judgment to consider the needs of our clients, colleagues, and the communities in which we operate. Each of us must take responsibility to explore, understand, and reflect on differences in culture, customs, holidays, language, business requirements, and the impact of our decisions on business dealings. Careful inquiry and dialog are required as is the need to adapt and be flexible, as appropriate, to best meet the needs of everyone concerned: business, clients, and employees.

Social:

Believe in winning the trust of the residents where you live
A strong community contributor
An excellent employer

Environmental:

We believe in doing right by where we live
Reducing our environmental footprint
Encouraging our suppliers and service partners to do the same

Economic: We believe in uplifting communities

1. Practicing economic sustainability for the benefit of the community and planet
2. Contributing to community prosperity as a major employer and through
3. sponsorships

Goal: To demonstrate a high level of corporate citizenship and social responsibility in all of your activities

The Importance of Being Unavailable

As business owners, we are often advised to prioritize our customers and cater to their needs. However, this doesn't mean that we should always be available to them at all times. Being overly accessible can do more harm than good to our business. To avoid this, setting boundaries and protecting your time is crucial. Here are some helpful tips to emphasize the importance of having clear-cut boundaries to maintain a healthy balance in your work and personal life.

Time To Focus and Plan

Having boundaries allows you to set up time dedicated to laying the foundation for your business. We all need time to think about our vision, how to serve our clients best and create systems to deliver excellence. We need to allow ourselves to have boundaries to successfully build a business to provide the service we promise to our clients.

Taking time out of your schedule to plan and organize your business can do wonders for your productivity. Dedicate a day or two each year to writing a complete business plan, and you'll have a clear sense of direction for the upcoming year. Additionally, setting aside 30 minutes weekly to plan and organize your schedule will help you stay on track and work more purposefully towards your business goals.

Time To Do the Vital Few

One of the biggest lessons we need to learn is that we do not need to do everything but rather be excellent at a few things. This is the Law of the Vital Few, or, as some know it, the 80/20 principle. For most of us, about 20% of our activities yield 80% of the revenue; this means we should spend most of our time on these vital few activities.

When we set boundaries, we have time to invest in these actions. After all, clients and businesses come from these actions; if we do not make time for these items, we will not have any business to focus on.

So, what are your vital few? Think about the things you, and you alone, must do, the items you cannot delegate. For me, those are my calls to clients, teaching classes, meeting one-on-one, and writing; I can delegate scheduling, editing, marketing, and such. Your vital few are the needle movers for you, the actions that bring in the revenue and must be done by you. Focus on these, and the business will follow.

Time To Reenergize and Think

We all need some time off to recharge our batteries. If we

asked our clients whether they would like us to take a break, most would probably say, "Yes." However, they also expect us to ensure they are cared for while we are away.

Maintaining the promised level of service is impossible if we are always available. Therefore, we must rest, refocus, re-energize, and think, and then we can return to work with renewed enthusiasm and energy.

A couple of years ago, one of my clients saw a massive growth in her business (about a 70% increase in revenue). When I asked her what the change was, she said she took time off; she went away and had someone cover her business and disconnected. She further expressed that this time away allowed her creativity and passion for her work to return; she felt excited and rested.

Time off is needed for success.

Others Valuing Your Time and Expertise

People want to work with other successful people. If we are always available, they will value our timeless and may not see us as experts in our field. If we have all the time in the world available, we must not have that much going on.

Have you ever heard of the doctor who was booking several months out? The restaurant that was so hard to get a reservation at? We see these as desirable and successful situations we want to be a part of. Allowing yourself to set boundaries with your time shifts the perspective that you are a success and that your time is valuable.

The truth is we hurt ourselves when we are too available.

We become burned out and lose focus, and small tasks fall through the cracks. Serving our clients does not mean we have always to be available. In truth, we can deliver better service when we implement boundaries. We must protect our time better; if we value our time, others will, too.

Work-Life Balance

The concept of work-life balance refers to the proportion of time you dedicate to working versus the time you devote to activities that matter to you beyond work, such as spending time with family and friends or engaging in hobbies. If work requires more time or attention, you may need more time to manage your other obligations or pursue your interests.

Many people commonly desire a better balance between work and personal life. However, it can be challenging to attain in reality. Sometimes, a high-pressure job can provide necessary financial support for a family. Conversely, a job can also negatively impact one's mental health, leading to exhaustion and strained personal relationships.

The concept of work-life integration, which combines personal and professional responsibilities in a mutually beneficial manner, has gained significant momentum. It is imperative to consider work in conjunction with other facets of our lives, such as our home and family lives, community involvement, and overall well-being.

Why is work-life balance important?

Improving your work-life balance is essential for your overall well-being, including your physical, emotional, and mental health. Research suggests that working extended hours may result in severe health problems such as "sleep deprivation, depression, excessive drinking, diabetes, memory loss, and heart disease." Unfortunately, these health issues can also worsen our work-life problems, leading to burnout and other undesirable consequences.

Finding the right balance between work and personal life is unique to each of us and can change over time as our responsibilities and priorities shift. It's an ongoing process of negotiation that requires careful consideration of how we allocate our time. Achieving a better work-life balance involves deciding what matters most to us, whether related to our job or personal life.

We have all experienced being overwhelmed by work demands, which can tip the work-life balance in one direction. Conversely, we may have unfulfilled aspirations and yearnings that tip the balance in the opposite direction. These factors gradually contribute to a general sense of disappointment and disinterest. How can you effectively allocate your time and energy to generate a sense of wholeness and engagement? What can help you present your best self and prevent burnout?

Work-life balance is often used to describe a trade-off. You balance the time spent on work projects versus time spent with family, friends, and personal interests.

- Self-help should be part of your daily regimen early in the morning, exercising and eating your best at each meal. This effort will prove to be one thing that creates consistency in what you do daily in work and life at a bare minimum.

- An early morning brisk walk can give you time to organize your day and mentally prepare to complete your task. Having a regular regimen with at least a piece of fruit in the morning for breakfast can be the difference between hitting your mark that day and falling short. Carving out time for family activities and possibly including your family in your daily regimen can be priceless. Planning a week or so each year with the family will be something you want to add to your yearly plan.

- There will be times when business may not be at its highest point; choose these times to work with your employees on what can be done to improve business. These times should be called planning times.

- Use the concept of the human race turning from hunters to gatherers to farmers to understand that in spring, you should plant all the seeds of what you want to grow during the summer. You should protect them from the heat, water them, and nurture them to thrive. Your fall time should be for harvesting, and your winter time should be made to consume what you have harvested; then, you'll be over again. The more you want, the more seeds you'll need to plant.

Achieving a healthy work-life balance can reduce stress and increase overall productivity.

Is your Business Sellable?

It's common for business owners to view their company as a profitable venture and believe that anyone would be fortunate to acquire it. While this may be accurate, most investors or entrepreneurs will only consider purchasing a business if specific criteria are met.

- Accessible processes that people can follow.
- Established systems for operations.
- A way to transfer the business from functions to proprietary processes.
- A way to transfer specialized business knowledge.

If you run everything in your company based on your knowledge and expertise but don't have a way to quickly transfer that knowledge to the new owner, your business likely cannot be sold. Fortunately, there are strategies you can use to make your business sellable.

Here are five strategies to make your business sellable

It is common for business owners to have exclusive knowledge about their company. However, this can make it difficult for a smooth ownership transition to occur. Therefore, it is important to systematically extract and document this specialized knowledge so that others can utilize it after the owner/seller has left the business.

Document the processes and procedures of each department.

CEOs alone cannot run businesses. Every department has its own specialized and sometimes exclusive processes and procedures. Usually, these are upheld by the owner/founder, who retains knowledge of everyone's roles and responsibilities - even if a crucial employee suddenly leaves. A purchaser must rely on something other than this prior knowledge. Instead, they require documented procedures to become acquainted with each department and effectively train new employees on standard company practices.

Document the business culture.

Each company has a unique business culture, and specific policies are in place to protect it. The culture may be constantly changing or unspoken. It is essential to bring stability to the company and sales by documenting the business culture and sharing the best actions to support it. When the previous owner or seller is no longer present, the new owner will want to ensure that the culture can thrive.

Bring in a consultant.

It is advisable to seek the assistance of a consultant. If a business owner still needs to document their processes and procedures or establish a knowledge transfer system, it would be beneficial to bring in a specialist who can extract, document, systematize, and implement these processes. For business owners who are mainly focused on selling their company, seeking the guidance of specialists to complete the documentation work is strongly recommended.

Add a co-partnership clause to the contract.

It is recommended that the buyer agrees to either co-partner or co-own the company for a certain period after the purchase. This will allow them to gain practical business management experience and use their preferred methods for documenting owner/operator processes to comprehend them better. Would you like to prepare your company for sale?

Understanding Your Business

A Guide to Management and Structure

What is HR?

Human Resources (HR) ensures the company complies with local, state, and federal employment laws, hires and retains new employees, trains employees, and supports their professional development. They are managing compensation and benefits.

As an owner or manager of a small business, you're accustomed to performing multiple responsibilities. Apart from being accountable for your business's strategic overview and administration, you're also extensively involved in daily duties, especially regarding human resources.

The responsibilities of HR, even for a small business, can be extensive. You may find yourself swamped with HR paperwork and administration, leaving little time to ensure everything is handled correctly and focus on expanding and improving your business. It's essential to have the time and resources to manage everything effectively.

Unsurprisingly, having enough time to do everything is one of the top five worries for small business owners.

That's a requirement to hand over HR responsibilities to someone else, or a group within your company is bound to arise. However, how can it determine the appropriate time to do so? And what steps should you take to establish a committed HR individual or team? Keep reading to learn more!

HR stands for human resources. The Society for Human Resource Organization) defines HR management as "management's" employees... to effectively meet an organization's goals."

The HR team is responsible for managing the complete employee journey, from the recruitment process to the end of the employment cycle, which can be through resignation, termination, or retirement. This involves overseeing all the aspects involved in between these stages.

This includes:

- Recruitment and retention
- Compensation and benefits management
- Payroll, including tax compliance
- Employee satisfaction, engagement, safety, and well-being
- Onboarding and offboarding
- Performance reviews
- Employee rewards and recognition

- Developing and maintaining employee resources such as training manuals and employee handbooks
- Creating company culture
- Employee participation and communication
- Training and development
- Time tracking and attendance
- Labor law compliance

When small businesses bring on their first employee, they immediately face HR challenges. While handling HR responsibilities and management duties may be feasible when you only have a few employees, the tasks can quickly become overwhelming as your business expands. It's easy to see how this can become too much for one person to handle.

What is Human Resource Management?

Human resources (HRM) management pertains to handling your staff regarding hiring, supervision, and other types of guidance and support. Among other responsibilities, HR personnel typically oversee:

- Hiring
- Performance management and reviews
- Employee development, motivation, and training
- Safety and wellness
- Benefits
- Communication between employees and management

HR carries a big responsibility. How people communicate, resolve conflicts, and collaborate in a company greatly influences its culture and environment. Although some small businesses may delegate a significant part of their human resources tasks to external providers, human resources must be addressed.

Human resources: The three basics

Small businesses often need to work on dealing with HR as they find it challenging to comply with laws and regulations. HR expert Jack Hayhow says businesses with less than 50 employees must cover the essential HR basics to meet their obligations. To avoid any legal implications, it is necessary to be flexible with HR policies and regulations.

Employee files

You must keep three specific files for each employee in your business. These files are:

- I-9 file: This form is used by the U.S. government to identify and verify that your employees are eligible to work in the U.S. Keep all of your employee I-9 files together in one file instead of under individual employee names.
- Employee general file: This is a file you create for your benefit. It contains any documentation associated with that employee you collected while with you. This includes resumes, reviews, disciplinary action, training, verify, evaluations, W-4 forms, payroll details, etc. You'll use this file often.
- Employee medical file: These files will contain notes from doctors, disability information, and any

medical information you have on an employee. Because you are dealing with medical information, you must protect and secure these files from others. That is why these are separate from general files. Be sure to keep them in a locked and secure place.

Employee handbook

An employee handbook is a necessary tool for any business. It serves two crucial purposes: outlining your expectations for your employees and safeguarding your business in the event of a conflict. Depending on the nature of your business, your employee handbook can be as straightforward or as complex as you like, but there are specific general approaches that you should consider. The Small Business Administration recommends that your handbook cover the following areas:

- **NDNA:** Not all businesses require signing non-disclosure agreements; only specific industries will benefit from it. If your company has confidential information that needs to be protected, then it's essential to use trade secrets as a safeguard.

- **Anti-discrimination policies:** It is important to discuss how to comply with the Americans With Disabilities Act and other employment discrimination laws if your business is in the United States.

- **Safety and security:** As a company, it is important to establish policies that promote a safe and secure work environment for your employees. This includes both physical safety and emotional well-being. It is advisable to discuss compliance with OSHA regulations, policies for handling lousy weather and emergencies, and the use of video surveillance systems. Additionally, your policies should clearly outline your expectations for your employees, such as using passwords on their computers, locking doors when necessary, and refraining from taking photos of their coworkers or the office with their mobile devices and sharing them online. Employees should also be encouraged to report threatening or concerning behavior to management.

- **Compensation and benefits:** Please clearly define the benefits that are mandatory by law and any unique benefits your business offers your employees. It is essential to inform them how to access these benefits and what is required to qualify. Additionally, it would be helpful to outline the salary or compensation levels and the necessary steps to attain them.

- **Work schedules, vacation, and leave:** Please explain your company's guidelines concerning schedules, tardiness, vacation and leave, absenteeism, special requests, and other similar matters. Also, if you permit remote work, I advise that you clearly communicate your expectations. Even if your organization offers a flexible work schedule, it is essential to document the expectations you have for your employees.

- **Standards of conduct:** It is essential to establish guidelines for employee conduct in the workplace, which may cover various areas such as attire, conduct, usage of computers and mobile devices during work hours, ethics, legal obligations, and similar topics. These guidelines should clearly outline the consequences of violating the established standards and be provided to employees in writing. This ensures a clear record of the expected code of conduct and the repercussions for not adhering to any issues.

- **General employment information:** Your company will establish its policies and procedures beyond legal requirements. It is important to precisely outline your policies related to work ethics, promotions, employee evaluations, dismissal, referrals, and employee records.

Ensure that your employee has been provided with a copy of the employee handbook, read it thoroughly, and signed a statement to acknowledge that they have received, read, and comprehended the handbook's contents. Keep the signed statement in their personnel file. Additionally, ensure that a copy of the handbook, either in digital or paper form, is easily accessible to all employees for future reference.

Display required posters

It may be necessary to display certain information in a location that is easily accessible, depending on the regulations of the country and state where your business is located. These requirements can vary depending on location, so seeking assistance from a local government agency or legal counsel is advisable to ensure compliance. Some companies offer pre-made poster packages specific to your area to simplify the process.

Human resources mistakes to avoid

An author, Margaret Jacoby, highlights five HR mistakes businesses frequently commit. These errors can be costly for small businesses long-term, resulting in monetary losses and time wastage.

- **Wrong hire:** Many small businesses hire anyone they can find to fill open positions. They lack the finances or resources to conduct thorough background checks or hiring processes.
  Unfortunately, there is no alternative to this; hiring

the wrong person can lead to issues and ultimately require finding a replacement.

- **No job definitions:** Many companies nowadays prefer "open-ended" job descriptions, but clearly communicating your expectations to your employees is more beneficial. Without a clear understanding of the specific job responsibilities, finding the right candidate for the position is impossible.

- **No performance documentation:** It is important to document all meetings, performance reviews, and issues, regardless of whether they are positive or negative. If an employee's performance is problematic, it should be discussed with them. It is advisable to create an improvement plan and to report it. These actions are crucial if an employee must be terminated or there is a legal action risk.

- **Ignoring employment laws:** You must comply with the employment regulations in the area where your business operates. Failing to do so, whether intentionally or unintentionally, will not shield you from any legal consequences or complications that may arise.

- **Improper classification:** Is your small business making use of contract employees? Have you verified that you have classified them correctly by the law? While many businesses opt for contract employees to save money and reduce complications, they may treat them as full- or part-time employees. The guidelines established by the IRS are stringent and could potentially cause issues down the line.

Mistakes like these set you on a serious path towards big problems.

Employee vs Independent Contractor (W2 vs 1099)

Misclassifying W-2 employees as 1099 contractors has severe penalties that can ruin an otherwise successful business.

What is a 1099 worker?

Workers who operate as independent contractors or freelancers are commonly referred to as "1099 workers," derived from the tax form they file with the Internal Revenue Service (IRS) at the end of the year. Since these workers are self-employed, businesses are not legally obligated to offer them benefits or include them in their payroll, as they are not technically employed by the company. Instead, 1099 workers are typically brought on board for a brief period to assist with a specific task or specialized project.

Opting for 1099 contractors instead of W-2 employees is a popular cost-cutting and legal liability avoidance strategy for many small businesses. However, there exist significant differences between the two workforce classifications. Correctly categorizing your workers is of utmost importance as the gig economy expands. Misclassifying W-2 employees as 1099 contractors can prove to be an expensive error as it may lead to severe penalties, lawsuits, or even imprisonment, which can halt your business operations.

What is the difference between W-2 and 1099 workers?

The distinction between a W-2 employee and a 1099 contractor may appear ambiguous, but the most critical factor is whether your business must deduct taxes from a worker's payments. If you categorize a worker as a W-2 employee, you are obligated to withhold Social Security tax, income tax, Medicare tax, and any state income taxes on behalf of the employee. If you classify workers as 1099 contractors, they are responsible for paying federal and state taxes themselves.

To help companies differentiate between and adequately classify the two types of workers, the Internal Revenue Service (IRS) provides guidance.

In most cases, a worker should be classified as a W-2 employee if:

- You (the business owner) control the details of how the work is performed.
- You provide office space, equipment, and supplies for the worker to complete tasks.
- You provide employee benefits, such as insurance, retirement plans, or vacation time.

Workers should be classified as 1099 contractors if:

- They control when and how they perform their work.
- They use their own equipment and supplies to complete tasks.
- They provide services to clients who pay them directly for their work.

What are the penalties if you misclassify employees?

Between 10% and 30% of employees, which translates to several million people across all industries, are wrongly categorized as 1099 contractors on a yearly basis. This misclassification allows companies to evade paying for various employee benefits, such as Medicare, Social Security, overtime, unemployment compensation, workers' compensation, vacation pay, and retirement plans. It is crucial for employers to correctly classify their workforce to avoid facing hefty fines and penalties. These penalties may include back wages due to non-compliance with the Federal Fair Labor Standards Act regarding minimum wage or overtime payment, a stop work order on the business, or even a complete ban on operating in a state or country. Businesses may also face a Form 1-9 audit by the Department of Homeland Security, U.S. Immigration and Customs Enforcement, and the Department of Labor, resulting in additional liabilities.

Business Structure

It's important to make a well-informed decision when selecting a business structure. Keep in mind that depending on where you are located, there may be limitations on changing your structure in the future. Additionally, this decision could have tax implications and lead to unintended dissolution or other complications.

What is a Sole proprietorship?

A sole proprietorship is an unincorporated business run solely by one individual proprietor. The word "sole" is sometimes used to designate a single item; it is most often defined as "lone" and "single." It is a business only available to one person, just like "Sole Proprietorship" implies.

Starting a sole proprietorship does not require any fees or forms to file. However, if you plan to use a business name other than your own, you must register a Doing Business As (DBA) name or Fictitious Business Name (FBN), depending on your state. You can begin your business immediately if your services do not require licensing. The owner of a sole proprietorship is entitled to all profits, but they are also responsible for the business's debts, losses, and liabilities. However, if you are starting a business with other people, you cannot establish a sole proprietorship. In that case, you will automatically form a general partnership instead.

What is a Partnership?

A partnership is a formal agreement between two or more parties to operate a business and distribute its profits. Partnership agreements come in several forms. In a partnership business, all partners share the liabilities and profits equally, while partners may have limited liability in other forms. In a for-profit venture undertaken by two or more individuals, there are three primary types of partnerships: general, limited, and limited liability.

General Partnership

A partnership agreement is the foundation for a general partnership, the simplest form of collaboration that does not require registering as a business entity with the state.

Under a general partnership, all partners share equal legal and financial liability. Each partner is personally accountable for the debts incurred by the partnership. Profits are also divided equally among the partners, as the partnership agreement specifies.

To ensure that the partnership runs smoothly, it is crucial to include an expulsion clause in the partnership agreement. This clause should outline the events that may lead to a partner being expelled from the partnership.

Limited Partnership (LP)

LPs are recognized as formal business entities by the state. One or more limited partners invest money in the business but are not responsible for managing it, while the general partner assumes full responsibility. In addition, a silent partner may be liable only for the amount invested; this partner typically does not participate in the partnership's day-to-day operations or management.

Limited Liability Partnership (LLP)

An LLP, or limited liability partnership, functions much like a general partnership, where all partners actively manage the business. However, an LLP limits the liability of each partner in terms of the actions of their fellow partners. While each partner is still fully responsible for the debts and legal liabilities of the business, they are not accountable for any mistakes or oversights made by their partners. This means that the assets of other partners are not at risk in case one partner is sued for malpractice. It's worth noting that LLPs are not allowed in every state and are often restricted to specific professions such as doctors, lawyers, and accountants.

Who Should Form a Partnership?

A partnership works well for companies with more than one owner, professional groups that want the benefits of a partnership but don't want to run the business (such as attorneys or doctors), or owners who want to try out a new business before creating a more formal business structure.

Entrepreneurs may decide on a partnership business structure if their business falls into one of the following categories:

- The business has multiple owners.
- It is a low-profit, low-risk business.
- It has a limited customer base.
- It is an enterprise transitioning from a hobby into a business.

What is an LLC?

An LLC or Limited Liability Company is a business structure that provides limited liability protection and pass-through taxation. Like corporations, the LLC is a separate entity from its owners, meaning that the owner's liability for business debts and liabilities is limited.

With an LLC, income is not taxed at the entity level; therefore, it is known for pass-through taxation. However, a tax return must be filed if the LLC has multiple owners. The LLC income or loss, as reported on the tax return, is then passed through to the members or owners of the LLC. These owners must report the income or loss on their tax returns and pay necessary taxes accordingly.

Benefits of an LLC

- liability protection for business owners and shareholders
- flexible business structure with a variety of trading options
- may result in a lower overall tax liability

Disadvantages of an LLC

- company accounts will be made public
- accounts are more complicated; even sole traders might need an account

What is a C Corporation?

The C corporation (c corp) is a popular type of corporation in the US, and it's not hard to see why. C corps provides unlimited potential for growth by selling stocks, which allows them to attract affluent investors. Additionally, there are no restrictions on the number of shareholders a C corporation can have.

Advantages of a C Corporation

There are many benefits of a C corporation. Below are just a few that stand out.

- Directors, officers, shareholders, and employees are protected by limited liability.
- The company has perpetual existence even if the owner departs.
- The company gains enhanced credibility and respect among suppliers and lenders.

- There is unlimited growth potential, thanks to the ability to sell stocks.
- There are no limits on shareholders. However, if the company has $10 million in assets and 500 shareholders, it must register with the SEC under the Securities Exchange Act of 1934.
- Certain tax advantages are available, such as tax-deductible business expenses.

Disadvantages of a C Corporation

Having unlimited growth comes with a few minor setbacks.

- Shareholders in C corporations face double taxation as revenue is taxed at the company level and again as shareholder dividends.
- Starting a C corporation can be expensive due to many fees associated with filing the Articles of Incorporation. Additionally, corporations must pay fees to the state where they operate.
- C corporations are subject to more government oversight and regulations than other companies. This is because of complex tax rules and the protection provided to owners from being responsible for debts, lawsuits, and other financial obligations.
- Unlike shareholders in an S corporation, those in a C corporation cannot deduct losses on their tax returns.

How to Form a C Corporation

- If your state allows it, select and reserve a legal name.

- Create and submit your Articles of Incorporation to the Secretary of State.
- Distribute stock certificates to the initial shareholders.
- Acquire a business license and any industry-specific certificates.
- Obtain an Employer Identification Number (EIN) by filing Form SS-4 or applying online through the IRS website.
- Obtain any additional ID numbers required by state and local government agencies. The specific requirements vary depending on your location, but generally, your business will be responsible for paying payroll taxes such as unemployment and disability, and you will need tax ID numbers for those accounts in addition to your EIN.

What is an S Corporation?

An S corp is a business that chooses to pass its profits and losses onto its shareholders, who must then pay taxes on that income. Unlike C corps, S corps are not required to pay corporate income tax.

S Corp Advantages

- Company directors, officers, shareholders, and employees are offered protection from unlimited liabilities.
- The profits and losses are reported by owners on their tax returns as pass-through taxation.

- Income is not taxed twice, as corporate income and dividend income are not subject to double taxation.
- The sale of stock shares can attract investors and provide investment opportunities for the company.
- The business has perpetual existence, even if the owner dies.
- The company has a once-a-year tax filing requirement, as opposed to C Corps, which must be filed quarterly.

S Corp Disadvantages

- To form an S corporation, you must be a US citizen or permanent resident. This differs from the C Corp and LLC, which don't have this requirement.
- An S corporation can have a maximum of 100 shareholders.
- Incorporating the business involves filing Articles of Incorporation with the state and paying the necessary fees. Additionally, there may be ongoing fees such as annual reports and franchise tax fees.
- Certain tax qualification obligations must be met for an S corporation. Please comply with these requirements to avoid accidentally leading to the termination of the corporation's status.
- The IRS pays closer attention to how payments to employees and shareholders are distributed in an S corporation. Salaries and dividends are taxed differently, which can lead to further scrutiny from the IRS.

How to Start and Form an S Corp

- Select a suitable name for your business and check if your state's Secretary of State allows you to reserve it.
- Create and submit your Articles of Incorporation to the Secretary of State.
- Distribute stock certificates to your initial shareholders.
- Apply for a business license and any other certifications required for your specific industry.
- Obtain an Employer Identification Number (EIN) by completing Form SS-4 or applying online at the Internal Revenue Service website.
- Obtain any other identification numbers necessary by state and local government agencies. Each jurisdiction has different requirements, but you will likely need to acquire tax ID numbers for accounts such as unemployment, disability, and payroll taxes in addition to your EIN.
- File the IRS form 2553 within 75 days of forming your corporation.

C Corporation vs. S Corporation

Both C and S corps provide limited liability protection and require the filing of Articles of Incorporation. They consist of shareholders, directors, and officers but differ in the complex area of taxation and corporate ownership.

C corporations face double taxation, while S corps are pass-through tax entities that avoid being taxed at the shareholder's level and again on shareholders' income taxes.

C corporations have no ownership restrictions, indicating their unlimited potential, but they are limited to having over 100 shareholders. On the other hand, S corps cannot be owned by C corps, other S corps, LLCs, partnerships, or many trusts. C corporations have no limitations on who or what can be a shareholder. Please refer to our business comparison chart for a comparison between corporations and LLCs.

Beneficial Ownership Information (BOI)

Starting **January 1, 2024**, almost every small business is required to file a Beneficial Ownership

Information (BOI) Report. This new reporting rule results from the Corporate Transparency Act, enacted

by Congress in 2021.

The purpose of beneficial ownership reporting is ultimately to help prevent the creation of

anonymous shell companies. Beneficial ownership reporting is an effort to help prevent money

laundering and other financial crimes by requiring those with control over businesses or legal entities to

provide identifying information. Because few U.S. states require companies to disclose information

about their beneficial owners, criminals and corrupt officials can hide their identities and launder money

through the U.S. via shell companies.

By requiring entities to report information about their beneficial owners to FinCEN, the

The Corporate Transparency Act aims to safeguard the U.S. financial system. Failure to comply with this

new law may result in penalties of up to $500 each day your business is out of compliance.

What is the rule?

Business entities, including corporations or limited liability companies established or registered

in the United States, must divulge their beneficial ownership information to FinCEN, per the BOI

Reporting Rule.

Who must comply?

The regulation typically pertains to national (registered in the United States) and international

(incorporated in foreign countries but authorized to conduct business in any U.S. jurisdiction)

enterprises. A helpful guideline to remember is that the regulation applies to any organization that has

submitted a registration document with a government agency, such as the Department of Corporations,

Secretary of State, or a comparable entity.

Are there exemptions?

The rule is by the Corporate Transparency Act of 2020, which outlines 23 types of entities that

are exempt from reporting requirements. These entities are already subject to significant oversight at the federal or state level. For instance, banks, credit unions, insurance companies, and any money

services transmitting business and money services business (MSB) registered with FinCEN and entities

registered with the Securities and Exchange Commission are among the examples.

What is a beneficial owner?

According to FinCEN, a beneficial owner is an individual who has significant influence over a

reporting company or possesses at least 25% ownership or control of the company, either directly or

indirectly.

How do businesses comply?

FinCEN requires companies to disclose their identity and provide information on their beneficial

owners, which includes the following details for each:

- Name
- Date of Birth
- Address
- Photo ID information and a copy of the ID

Beneficial owners have the option to provide their information directly to FinCEN. In such cases, they

will be given a "FinCEN identifier", which reporting companies can use instead of submitting the

required beneficial ownership details for that individual. FinCEN will continue to provide guidance and

instructions on filing reports and how businesses can comply with the new rule until its effective date.

When must businesses be compliant?

Starting from January 1, 2024, the rule will come into effect. Reporting companies will be given
a year to file their initial reports. For companies that are established after the effective date, they must
comply within 30 days of their creation or registration.

Insurance & Bonds

Insurance covers your losses on your behalf, while surety bonds ensure payment to a third party. The main distinction between insurance and surety bonds is that insurance compensates for damages in a claim, whereas a bonding firm assures that your responsibilities are met.

Business insurance is a safety net for your business, enabling you to withstand financial hardships and bounce back from any losses incurred.

As a cleaning business owner, you encounter various hazards daily, ranging from property damage and theft to accidents and legal action. These hazards can arise from different origins, such as clients, workers, and subcontractors, and can lead to substantial financial setbacks for your business.

When you invest in business insurance, you can safeguard your cleaning business from potential losses. With business insurance, you won't have to bear the costs of legal claims, damage to property, or any other financial setbacks with your funds. In essence, business insurance offers assurance and protection over your assets — something that cannot be priced.

Starting a cleaning business can be daunting, especially in

the early days when expenses seem endless. Once you factor in cleaning supplies, marketing, employees, software, and paying yourself, the thought of incurring additional costs is overwhelming. However, it is crucial to remember that every expense is worth it in the long run.

Not having business insurance can put you in a tough financial spot in case of unforeseen events or legal liabilities. If you believe that such situations won't happen to you, think again and reflect on the following scenarios:

Legal Liabilities: It's important for owners of cleaning businesses to be aware that they may face serious trouble in case of injury to a customer or employee. If you don't have business insurance, you may be required to personally cover the expenses of medical bills and any other damages. Business insurance can provide you with the necessary protection against legal liabilities.

Damages to Customer's Property: As a cleaning business owner, you could be held accountable for any harm caused to a customer's belongings, like damaged furniture or stained carpet. To alleviate the financial burden, business insurance can cover these damages, saving you from paying for them out of your own pocket.

Loss of Income: Cleaning business owners may face difficulties recovering from losses caused by unexpected events such as natural disasters or theft without proper business insurance. Business insurance can help owners restore their cleaning businesses as quickly as possible by providing coverage for lost income.

Employee Injuries: If an employee sustains injuries while working, the cleaning business owners may be held accountable for paying for their medical expenses and lost income. To avoid out-of-pocket expenses, business insurance can assist with covering these costs.

Lawsuits: If a customer or employee claims that you or your employees acted negligently or committed fraud, it is possible for cleaning business owners to be sued. However, if you have business insurance, it can assist in covering the cost of legal fees and settlements, so you don't have to pay out of pocket.

General Liability Insurance:

Your business can be protected against third-party claims of bodily injury or property damage by a particular type of insurance. It covers medical expenses, court costs, and damages up to the policy limit. This insurance is of utmost importance for cleaning businesses as it covers any accidents that might occur while cleaning someone else's property.

Product Liability Insurance:

Product liability insurance, also called cleaning supplies insurance, safeguards your cleaning business against damages or injuries that may arise from your cleaning products. This type of insurance can cover legal fees, medical bills, and other costs associated with product liability claims.

Workers' Compensation Insurance:

Workers' compensation insurance is mandatory for cleaning businesses that employ one or more people. This type of insurance covers medical expenses and lost wages for employees who get injured while working.

Commercial Property Insurance:

In case of damage or theft, your business's physical assets, such as equipment, supplies, and inventory, will be covered by Commercial Property insurance. In the case of cleaning businesses, this insurance can also compensate for loss of income caused by a fire or other covered event that disrupts normal operations.

Commercial Auto Insurance:

Suppose your cleaning company uses vehicles that belong

to the business. In that case, it's crucial to have commercial auto insurance to safeguard your business in case of an accident, theft, or damage to the vehicle. This type of insurance can provide coverage for both the driver and the vehicle and any harm done to other individuals or property. It can also offer protection for rental and personal vehicles used by employees for business purposes.

Hired and Non-Owned Insurance:

Hired and non-owned insurance is an extra attachment to a general liability policy that provides coverage for workers or contractors who use their own or rented vehicles for business purposes. If you have either W-9 employees or 1099 contractors working for your company, and they operate their car during your company's time, your company may still be held responsible. However, it is important to note that Hired and Non-Owned Insurance cannot substitute personal auto insurance. If an employee or contractor causes an accident while driving their vehicle, their auto insurance will still be the primary coverage for the accident.

Business Interruption Insurance:

If a covered event like a natural disaster prevents your cleaning business from operating, this insurance can provide financial compensation for any lost income. Additionally, it may cover any temporary business relocation expenses that arise.

Professional Liability Insurance:

This insurance type is also called Errors and Omissions Insurance. It provides coverage for claims that may arise from negligence or errors committed by your cleaning business while delivering services.

LICENSES AND REGISTRATIONS

Your business structure and location determine the process of registering your business. Once you have these details, the registration process becomes easier. Registering your business name with the local and state governments is usually required for small businesses.

In certain situations, registration may not be necessary. You may not require registration if you operate your business under your legal name. However, remember that you may lose out on personal liability protection, legal advantages, and tax benefits by not registering your business. Mostly, businesses do not need to register with the federal government to establish legal status, except for obtaining a federal tax ID. Some small businesses register for trademark protection or tax-exempt status with the federal government.

After forming your business, file with the United States Patent and Trademark Office if you wish to trademark your product, brand, or business name. If you want your nonprofit corporation to have tax-exempt status, ensure that you register your business as a tax-exempt entity with the IRS. You must file form 2553 with the IRS to establish an S corp.

If your company is structured as an LLC, corporation, partnership, or nonprofit corporation, it will likely need to register with any state where it conducts business activities.

Generally, you are deemed to be conducting business activities in a state when:

- Your business has a physical presence in that state.
- You frequently have in-person meetings with clients there.
- A significant portion of your company's revenue is derived from that state.
- Any of your employees work in that state.

Some states allow you to register online, while others require you to file paper documents in person or by mail.

Most states mandate that you register with either the Secretary of State's office, a Business Bureau, or a Business Agency to operate a business legally. Before filing, if your business falls under the categories of LLC, corporation, partnership, or nonprofit corporation, you must have a registered agent in your state.

Your company requires someone to receive official papers and legal documents on its behalf, which is where a registered agent comes in. It's important to note that the registered agent must be in the same state where your company is registered. Some business owners use a registered agent service instead of handling this responsibility.

You may need to establish your business in one state and then apply for a foreign qualification in other states where your business is active if you conduct business activities in multiple states and your LLC, corporation, partnership, or nonprofit corporation is involved.

When you establish your business in a particular state, that state will consider it domestic. However, all other states will regard it as a foreign business. It needs to undergo foreign qualification to inform a state that a foreign business is active there. Businesses that have undergone foreign qualification typically have to pay taxes and annual report fees in both their state of formation and the states where they have undergone foreign qualification. You must file a Certificate of Authority with the state to undergo foreign qualification. Besides this, many states also require a Certificate of Good Standing from the state where your business is formed. Each state has a different filing fee for foreign qualification, which varies depending on the business structure. It is best to check with state offices to learn about foreign qualification requirements and fees.

Registering your business can be less than $300, but the fees may differ based on your state and business structure.

You will generally require the following information:

- Business name
- Business address
- Ownership, management structure, or directors
- Registered agent details
- Number and value of shares (if you're a corporation)

The documents you require and the information that needs to be included in them will vary depending on your state and business structure.

It's important to note that registering your DBA (trade name or fictitious name) may be required in some states. You should check with your state government office to find out what's required in your area. Generally, you do not need to register with county or city governments when forming your business. However, if your business is an LLC, corporation, partnership, or nonprofit corporation, you may need to apply for licenses and permits from the county or city. Some counties and cities also require you to register your DBA — a trade or fictitious name — if you use one.

To ensure compliance with registration, licensing, and permitting requirements, it is essential to check the websites of your local governments. After registering, certain states may ask for reports to be submitted shortly after that, depending on your business structure. In addition, you might be required to submit additional documentation to your state or franchise tax board, usually known as Initial Reports or Tax Board registration. These filings are typically due within 30-90 days of registration. To see if this applies to you, consult your local tax office or franchise tax board.

CERTIFICATIONS

Professional certifications unlock several opportunities. However, have you ever considered obtaining a certification for your small business? What are the advantages of having a small business certification, and what are the different certifications available?

- The U.S. Small Business Administration (SBA) is a government agency that extends support and opportunities to small businesses and entrepreneurs. It offers certification programs like the Woman Owned Small Business (WOSB) Program, HUBZone Program, and 8(a) Business Development Program, which allow businesses to qualify for specific government contracts.

- Several minority-centered organizations, such as the National Minority Supplier Development Council, provide certifications that help minority entrepreneurs secure new businesses from the private sector.

- Both government and industry organizations, including state and city governments, offer various certifications. These certifications often lead to more minor contracts limited to their jurisdiction, such as Small Business Entity (SBE).

WOMEN OWNED SMALL BUSINESS (WOSB) AND WOMEN'S BUSINESS ENTERPRISE (WBE) CERTIFICATION

The Small Business Administration (SBA) in the United States provides two types of certifications for women-owned businesses. The Women-Owned Small Business (WOSB) Certification gives access to federal contracts that are competitive and exclusive. To qualify for this certification, the business must be owned by one or more women who manage it, and women must own 51% of the business.

The certification for Women's Business Enterprise (WBE) makes a business eligible to work on government and private sector contracts. The WBE certification requirements are similar to those of the WOSB certification, which means that a woman must hold the highest position in the company and be actively involved in daily management. By obtaining the WBE certification, you can achieve your business development goals by gaining access to new contracts, networking opportunities, as well as training and education programs. The certification process for WOSB or WBE can be initiated by working with any of the four SBA-approved third-party certifiers or through self-certification with the SBA.

Minority Business Enterprise (MBE) Certification

It can be highly beneficial for minority-owned businesses to obtain a Minority Business Enterprise (MBE) Certification, as it can provide access to private sector and corporate contracts, networking opportunities, searchable supplier databases, and specialized financing. To be eligible for this certification, minority business owners must possess at least a 51% ownership stake in the company and satisfy other qualifying criteria.

B Corp Certification

B Corps is a for-profit organization that must adhere to strict social and environmental performance standards, accountability, and transparency. Becoming a B Corp Certified company is similar to obtaining an organic certification for a local farm - it demonstrates your company's commitment to social and environmental responsibility.

By obtaining B Corp Certification, your company will be associated with well-known organizations such as Ben & Jerry's, Patagonia, and Warby Parker. As 66% of global consumers are willing to pay more to support companies dedicated to sustainability, this certification can set your company apart. It can serve as a valuable marketing tool to attract new clients and potential investors, and it also provides access to other B Corp members and networking opportunities.

Veteran Owned Small Business (VOSB) and Service-Disabled Veteran-Owned Small Business (SDVOSB) Certification

Certification can be crucial for veteran-owned small businesses to access prime federal government contracts and subcontracts through set-asides. The federal government has regulations to ensure that small businesses get a fair share of work in the federal market, including setting aside a percentage of their contracts for veteran-owned small businesses each year.

The process for obtaining Veteran Owned Small Business (VOSB) and Service-Disabled Veteran-Owned Small Business (SDVOSB) Certifications can be complicated as no single government body or third party manages the certifications. Register with VetBiz Registry, a veteran business database, to obtain certification as a veteran-owned business. If you are service-disabled, you will also need a disability status letter from the VA during the application process.

Once your company has obtained VOSB or SDVOSB Certification, you can participate in the U.S. Department of Veterans Affairs (VA) Veterans First Contracting Program, which grants access to set-aside contracts with the VA. To become eligible for government contracts, you must register with the Central Contractor Registration (CCR) after registering with the VA. Lastly, if you are interested in pursuing larger contracts with the federal government, you should also register with the General Services Administration (GSA).

Small Disadvantaged Business Certification 8(a)

In 2008, the SBA introduced the Small Disadvantaged Business Certification. Unlike the regular certification process, businesses are not required to apply and wait for approval. Instead, they can self-represent their status. The main eligibility criteria for this certification is that the company should be owned by disadvantaged individuals who may be socially or economically disadvantaged.

It is worth noting that having this certification can make businesses eligible for other SBA programs, such as the SBA's 8(a) Business Development Program.

HUBZone business certification

The HUBZone program aims to promote small businesses in historically underutilized areas by awarding them at least 3% of federal contract dollars annually. To qualify for the HUBZone program, a small business must meet specific criteria such as being located in a HUBZone, having at least 30% of its employees living in a HUBZone, and being 51% owned and controlled by U.S. citizens, a Community Development Corporation, an agricultural cooperative, a Native Hawaiian organization or an Indian tribe. The SBA is constantly working to improve the HUBZone program for applicants by improving decision-making turnaround time, streamlining applications, and expanding early engagement. If you want to apply for HUBZone business certification, you can do so on the SBA's website. A HUBZone certification has no time limit, but the business must recertify for the program once a year. Additionally, a review of your business will be required every three years.

Conclusion

The preceding chapters have comprehensively covered what a small business needs and

highlighted the key elements contributing to its success. Passion and discipline are key to achieving

success in anything you do. You should pursue your passions because they bring you joy, not because

they feel like work. Pursuing your passions can lead to more excellent knowledge and an expanded

understanding of people, places, and things. Whenever you encounter someone, embrace them, listen , and ask them more questions than you give advice. Learn from your own mistakes and the mistakes of

others. Pushing yourself to the breaking point is sometimes necessary, but remember why you started.

Be someone other than the person who always points out flaws or deficiencies. Instead, be the person

who offers solutions and options for resolution.

Remember, every day is an opportunity to learn something new in business. The education

never ends, but success is achievable if you focus on your passion and what you love. Many people
have succeeded in following their dreams, so be one of those passionate and transparent business
owners who prioritize integrity and giving back.

Growing your business requires continuous daily improvement; you should strive to know more
about what you do. Embracing mistakes and failures is a critical component of learning and progress.
You can always move forward with your business, even when times get tough. Revisit why you started
your business; this will reignite your passion and keep you going.

Starting a commercial cleaning business can be challenging, but learning about people, places,
and your surroundings is an excellent opportunity. Feel free to communicate with others in the same
business. This will provide valuable insight into planning, growing, and profiting from your business.

Take the information in this book and use it to catapult yourself to new heights. Always
remember, "It's not all about cleaning". Thank you for reading.

www.ingramcontent.com/pod-product-compliance
Lightning Source LLC
Chambersburg PA
CBHW020624160726
47991CB00002BA/917